To: _____

From: _____

Published by Sourcebooks Casablanca, an imprint of Sourcebooks, Inc.
P.O. Box 4410, Naperville, Illinois 60567-4410
(630) 961-3900
Fax: (630) 961-2168
www.sourcebooks.com

ISBN-13: 978-1-4022-1093-8
ISBN-10: 1-4022-1093-0

Printed and bound in the United States of America
SP 10 9 8 7 6 5 4 3 2 1

COUPONS
for the
GR⊙⊙M

COUPONS

for the

GR⌾⌾M

Honey—too much wedding planning! Drop everything and come out **dancing with me.**

GR⬤⬤M

Eat in or go out—tonight it's **just the two of us.** That means no wedding planners, no cell phones, and **no checklists.**

Tonight we eat at **my favorite restaurant.** The only seating decision you have to make is whether you want to sit across from or **next to me!**

COUPONS
for the
GRM

This coupon entitles me to a **quiet afternoon** at home with you, watching the **sporting event of my choice.**

COUPONS *for the* GR⊙⊙M

Let's get outside! Hiking, walking, or biking,
it's your choice. If we get lost in the woods,
at least we have each other!

COUPONS for the GROOM

Take a break from bridal showers—tonight's our night to play cards or our favorite board games. I'll give you six kisses for every game you win (or lose)!

COUPONS
for the
GROOM

No fancy reception food tonight—
with this coupon, it's **burgers and fries**
and a **milkshake with two straws!**

GRO💍M

We're going to **grow old together,** but that doesn't mean we can't **play like kids!** If you drop the fabric swatches and invitation samples, I'll take you out for a **night at the arcade.**

We don't have to go into "wedding mode" tonight! Join me for a **sunset picnic** on the beach. Bring your appetite but **shoes are optional.**

COUPONS *for the* GROOM

Instead of working on the guest list tonight, let's have a **night out** on the town! The **drinks are on me.**

COUPONS

for the

GROOM

No travel arrangements necessary—let's go out back and **watch the stars together.**

COUPONS *for the* GROOM

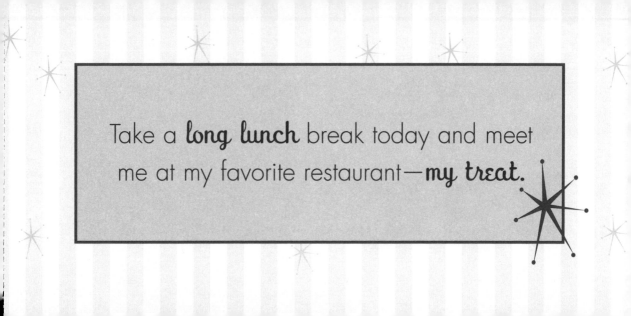

Take a **long lunch** break today and meet me at my favorite restaurant—**my treat.**

COUPONS

for the

GR⬭⬭M

Put aside the contracts and guest lists!
I'm redeeming this coupon for
a *romantic boat ride together.*

GROOM

Instead of shopping for wedding favors, let's go to the **batting cages** and hit one **out of the park!**

No parties tonight—there's **nothing better** than an evening at home together, unwinding in **each other's arms.**

COUPONS
for the
GRM

When things get hectic, this coupon is **good for one phone call** to tell me how much **you love me.**

COUPONS
for the
GR⊙⊙M

Now that we've got the wedding music planned, **let's go to a concert** together—we can scream, dance, and **buy T-shirts** as a souvenir!

COUPONS for the GR⊙⊙M

I've had a stressful week at work and I'm not ready to sit down and look at wedding stuff. Instead, can we **just go bowling?**

COUPONS

for the

GR⊙⊙M

Let's go to the bookstore **together** and find some reading material for **our honeymoon.** If you buy me the book I want, **I'll return the favor!**

I know that the **spark** between us will never fade—let's **light sparklers** in the backyard tonight. I'd love to get you **alone in the dark!**

Limousine rides are cool, but tonight we're going to the **carnival** for some fun and games. **Watch out for kisses** when we get to the top of the Ferris wheel!

COUPONS

for the

GROM

With this coupon, you'll **take a break** from guest lists and **give me one kiss** for every person we plan to invite. Suddenly, I wish we had invited **more people!**

COUPONS *for the* GROOM